Facts About the Amazon River Dolphin

By Lisa Strattin

© 2016 Lisa Strattin

Revised © 2019

Facts for Kids Picture Books by Lisa Strattin

Harlequin Macaw, Vol 34

Downy Woodpecker, Vol 37

Frilled Lizard, Vol 39

Purple Finch, Vol 48

Poison Dart Frogs, Vol 50

Giant Otter, Vol 57

Hornbill, Vol 67

Dwarf Lemur, Vol 73

Giant Squirrel, Vol 76

Star Tortoise, Vol 79

Sign Up for New Release Emails Here

http://LisaStrattin.com/subscribe-here

Monthly Surprise Box

http://KidCraftsByLisa.com

All rights reserved. No part of this book may be reproduced by any means whatsoever without the written permission from the author, except brief portions quoted for purpose of review.

All information in this book has been carefully researched and checked for factual accuracy. However, the author and publisher makes no warranty, express or implied, that the information contained herein is appropriate for every individual, situation or purpose and assume no responsibility for errors or omissions. The reader assumes the risk and full responsibility for all actions, and the author will not be held responsible for any loss or damage, whether consequential, incidental, special or otherwise, that may result from the information presented in this book.

All images are free for use or purchased from stock photo sites for commercial use.

Some coloring pages might be of the general species due to lack of available images.

I have relied on my own observations as well as many different sources for this book and I have done my best to check facts and give credit where it is due. In the event that any material is used without proper permission, please contact me so that the oversight can be corrected.

Contents

INTRODUCTION 7

CHARACTERISTICS 9

APPEARANCE 11

LIFE STAGES 13

LIFE SPAN 15

SIZE 17

HABITAT 19

DIET 21

FRIENDS AND ENEMIES 23

SUITABILITY AS PETS 25

RIVER DOLPHIN TOY 38

MONTHLY SURPRISE BOX 39

INTRODUCTION

These Amazon River Dolphin are warm-blooded mammals designed for life in freshwater. They are found in South America along the Amazon River and branches of this river. The Amazon flows through the countries of Colombia, Brazil, Bolivia, Peru, and Ecuador. In these countries where Spanish or Portuguese is the main language, this animal is called a "boto" or a "bufeo."

There are five species of river dolphin in the world, and this is the biggest one. They are closely related to porpoises and toothed whales. Unlike most other dolphin, however, they do not live in large pods, or family groups. Most individuals live by themselves except when they seek a partner for mating purposes.

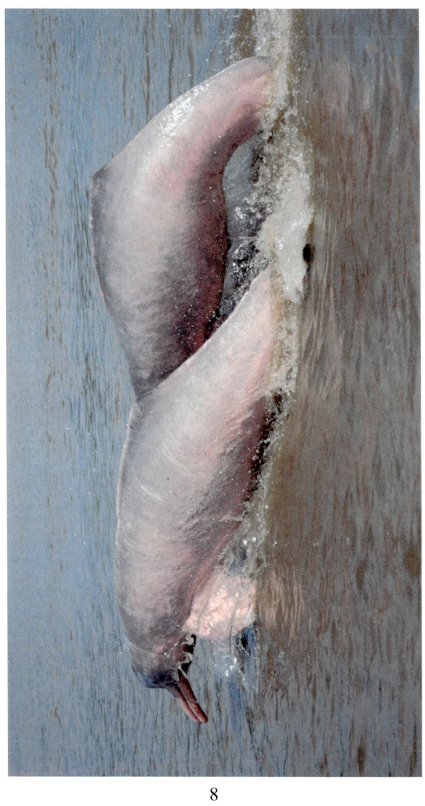

CHARACTERISTICS

The amazon River Dolphin are very intelligent and playful. They may appear curious and friendly towards humans. They do not see very well, so instead of sight they use sound waves to guide them while swimming and hunting for food. This is called "echolocation."

They swim underwater but must come to the water surface every so often to breathe. Sometimes they will even leap out of the water and dive back in. They take short naps underwater. They communicate with other dolphin through a series of clicks and other sounds. They are unusual because they can turn their heads to look left and right.

APPEARANCE

The first thing you notice is the pink and grey colored skin. Instead of the large dorsal fin that you would see in other dolphins, this species has only a small ridge in the middle of their backs. They have a blow hole on the top of their head for breathing. Their heads have a melon-like shape, they have small eyes and a long thin snout.

The shape of their mouth makes them seem like they are smiling. When they open their mouths, you can see a row of teeth on both upper and lower jaws. Instead of arms they have flippers and instead of legs they have a single powerful flat tail.

LIFE STAGES

An adult female will carry a baby inside her for as long as 12 months. When she gives birth, the baby pushes out of her body tail-first. Once fully born, the new baby is called a calf. Its mother will bring it up to the water surface to take its first breath of air. Calves nurse by drinking their mother's milk for the next 4 months. After that, their teeth grow big enough so that they can eat fish like their mother does.

Even once the calf is weaned and no longer relies on its mother for food it stays close by her for several months or even years. The calf learns by watching its mother and then repeating her actions. It grows bigger and becomes more independent. Once it becomes an adult it can live on its own.

LIFE SPAN

On average the Amazon River Dolphin lives 15 years. Some individuals may live much longer, perhaps even reaching 30 years.

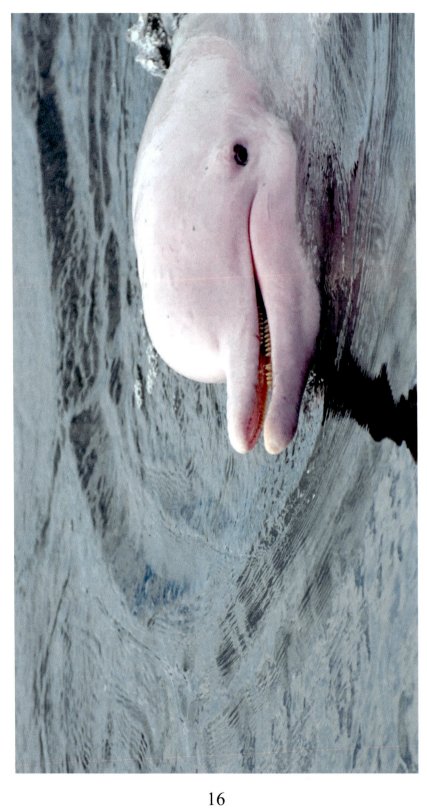

SIZE

These are very large mammals measuring from 6 to 8 feet from their nose to their tail. That is longer than many adult humans. Males are bigger than the females in size.

HABITAT

While many dolphin live in salt water oceans, this species lives only in freshwater rivers. These rivers are not very deep but they can still be dark or muddy-looking because of all the leaves and sticks falling into them from the surrounding rainforests.

DIET

These animals eat a diet of freshwater fish and crustaceans. Crustaceans are creatures that have a hard outer shell. Examples are shrimp, crayfish, and crabs.

FRIENDS AND ENEMIES

Other dolphin can be considered friends of the Amazon River Dolphin.

An adult can usually fight or swim fast enough to get away from danger. However, a young calf faces many enemies in the rainforest environment, including a jaguar or leopard, a caiman (similar to a crocodile), or an anaconda snake.

SUITABILITY AS PETS

This is not an animal that is suitable to be a house pet. It may seem friendly but it is still a wild animal that can bite and hurt you. It is too heavy for you to be able to lift it up. If you remove it from the water it will soon die because its skin will dry out. The best idea is to leave them alone in the wild where they are happy to live.

COLOR ME

COLOR ME

COLOR ME

COLOR ME

COLOR ME

COLOR ME

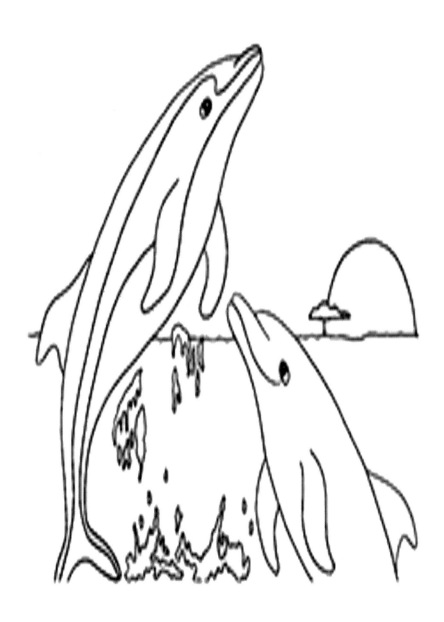

COLOR ME

COLOR ME

COLOR ME

COLOR ME

Please leave me a review here:

http://lisastrattin.com/Review-Vol-166

For more Kindle Downloads Visit Lisa Strattin Author Page on Amazon Author Central

http://amazon.com/author/lisastrattin

To see upcoming titles, visit my website at LisaStrattin.com– all books available on kindle!

http://lisastrattin.com

RIVER DOLPHIN TOY

You can get one by copying and pasting this link into your browser:

http://lisastrattin.com/RiverDolphinToy

MONTHLY SURPRISE BOX

Get yours by copying and pasting this link into your browser

http://KidCraftsByLisa.com

Made in the USA
Las Vegas, NV
06 December 2020